SPIRITUAL ENCOUNTERS

BY

SHIV MATHUR

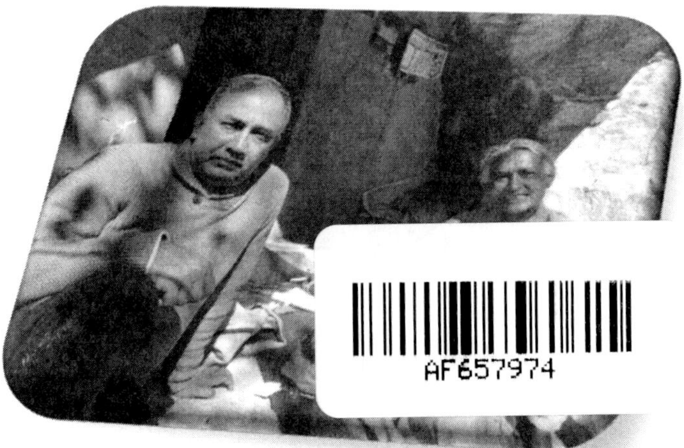

MEETING THE HIMALAYAN YOGIS

PREFACE

1. I am grateful to my parents and God, who have brought me up and given me a direction in this life to move on a path of self realization and truthfulness.

2. In the journey of this soul which came to this body, the experiences have been interesting and worth sharing. That is why I thought that consolidating them in this book will provide some good food for thought and also an interesting material for the eyes.

3. I will keep my preface short as this is my second book, and I would be happy if the soul reading this book has also read the previous book. I would like to dedicate this book to my parents.

4. This is a colourful book with images taken by me during my travels. I hope it will provide a gripping reading and stimulating experience to the spiritually inquisitive souls.

**My Father –
KRISHNA MOHAN MATHUR**

My Mother –
Late. MOHINI MATHUR

TABLE OF CONTENTS

CHAPTER-1

BACKGROUND

1.1 I was born on the 09th of March 1966 at Varanasi, India. I did my schooling in Kota, Rajasthan. Thereafter, I did my B.Tech in Electrical Engineering from NIT Warangal in 1989. I got married in Oct 1991. After completing my engineering, I joined the Indian Navy and served there for 16 years. I took pre-mature retirement from the Navy in Oct 2005. I then worked in the corporate sector in companies like IBM, Tulip Telecom, Tata Teleservices, Tata Communications, Saudi Telecom, Juniper Network and finally Reliance Jio.

1.2 It was in the year 2010, that a thought appeared about the Vedas, the ancient scriptures of Bharat (India). It was a curiosity about the knowledge therein which was supposed to be all encompassing and ultimate. Along with this, there was another curiosity about the Himalayan Yogis. Despite living in such harsh conditions, how are they able to attain true knowledge and eternal bliss? I then started looking for some information, as until then, I was just not into any kind of spirituality, yoga or religious inclinations. I found a book titled "A Search in Secret India" by Paul Brunton. This colourful book gave me some ideas about the spiritual world and the existence of some realized Yogis in Bharat.

1.3 In the year 2011, I went through some difficult situations in my relationships, which lead me to start questioning about the purpose of life. Questions like – Does anyone really belong to us, what are we chasing, for whom are we living such a life trying to strive for more and more of materialistic acquisitions, why are we always trying to please others and when the time comes same people will turn their back. As the introspection started, many beliefs and myths got shattered.

1.4 Life was on a fast track, chasing a big target aligned to our financial goals. To make it more difficult, we faced uncertain economic conditions and an equally challenging job market. There was not really much time left for introspection. However, I am a strong family and home loving person. In 2013-2014, I had to be in Jakarta, Indonesia for about five months, for a project for my company. My family had to be in India. While living alone in Jakarta, I realized that life is just not about money. It is important to be with your family. To me, family was always a priority and family was also my driving force to work hard and excel in order to fulfill the family goals and responsibilities. Then in 2015, I went alone for a job to Riyadh, Saudi Arabia. Same realization happened, that chasing money is futile, and one should be content with what they can attain without compromising on certain priorities in life. I realized that happiness was in living together as a family and not by earning more and then spending even more on the materialistic acquisitions. This is a very sensitive situation, and sometimes one has to compromise and go through a grind so as to meet one's aspirations or responsibilities towards the family. It is a delicate balance that needs to be maintained. Notwithstanding the good tax free salary package I had in Riyadh, I took the decision to return to India, even though I had spent only two months in that new job in Saudi Telecom. I was lucky that I could get another job as soon as I returned to India.

1.5 **The Spiritual Calling** : Towards the end of 2015, I got a strong urge to visit Rishikesh, which is literally the gateway to the Land of Gods. It is also a place where many seekers from across the globe come looking for food for the soul. Rishikesh is also known as the Yog capital of the world. Here onwards started the quick march on my spiritual path, more visibly as well as more vigorously.

CHAPTER-2

SPIRITUAL ENCOUNTERS

2.1 As the urge to visit Rishikesh was so strong, I booked my train tickets from Mumbai to Haridwar (Haridwar is the train station and Rishikesh is another 25 kms away by road). This was sometime around 20th of November 2015. I had searched for a suitable ashram in Rishikesh and found one by the name "Yog Niketan" to be more appropriate for my two-week stay.

2.2 The train reached Haridwar, and lo and behold, I could feel the divinity in the air. The view of the hills from the railway station itself was like a movie trailer, which left me spellbound. The movie had just begun. I reached the ashram after an hour's ride from Haridwar. (Hari means God and dwar means gateway). Though by now I have stayed in quite a few ashrams in Rishikesh, I still consider

RISHIKESH

this ashram as one of the best. It is perched on top of the hill right next to the famous Ram Jhula tempo stand. It is right there where there is all the hustle and bustle, but strategically placed so that it is secluded & serene, and can still provide a bird's eye view of everything, including the divine river Ganges. I have another chapter just on the ashrams; therefore, through this book you will get to see a threadbare analysis of quite a few ashrams. This will help you in taking a decision about choosing the one appropriate for you.

2.3 I was not interested in doing yog asanas or the morning meditation, which were part of the ashram routine. One is free to join the ashram routine and there is no extra cost for the same. My only participation was in the three meals which were part of the daily tariff. I had embarked on a search in the wilderness. I had switched ON all my radars, antennae, communications devices, and the propulsion system. Basically, all my sensory organs and the limbs were operating at their highest efficiency, looking for the target I had set out for.

2.4 Rishikesh is one place on earth which is very unique, and I can bet that there is no other place on earth which is so vibrant and divine. It is a melting pot of cultures from all over the world. This place totally uplifts you to a different plane. People get emotional, they cry, they get purified, and much more. Even the small shops lined up on the way to Ram Jhula offer numerous affordable and attractive titbits. I can also call it a world of spiritual illusion. The westerners are all dressed in the traditional Indian costumes, giving a mesmerizing look and appeal. I think I can actually write an entire book on Rishikesh, Eureka !!! I will move on to the topic on which the book is being written, though I have a habit of digressing. Never mind, I do converge at the end of every diversion.

2.5 The first surprise I had was that I could only sleep for four hours every night. The second night, I tried shifting my time to go to bed, but still I could not sleep for more than four hours. While lying in the bed, I decided to start searching online for the existence of any great yogis in Rishikesh. Mr. Google popped up a yogi who looks very scintillating and dashing. It was none other than Tatwale Baba ji. There was a short 32 page book listed on a website about him. He had lived in a cave somewhere around Rishikesh. Hence, I started the treasure hunt, as I had found my first target. Next day I hired a bicycle and went around hunting for Tatwale Baba's cave. As there is a saying that it is dark underneath the lantern, I realized that many locals were blissfully unaware of the existence of this cave. They are too occupied with their daily chores. In Rishikesh, you have the seekers searching for that unknown, and the other ones are the locals who are the providers.

Though I feel they are inherently blessed to be born there and live there. Maybe you have to be born elsewhere to discover a place inhabited by the locals. The locals remain ignorant or they are probably used to the existence of those places which otherwise look exotic to outsiders. Probably, this is a human tendency everywhere. While the locals exploit these places commercially, the outsiders exploit them differently, in this case, spiritually.

2.6 **The first ENCOUNTER** : Finally, I got a clue from one Sadhu, who is originally from the Netherlands, but has been living in Rishikesh for the last 30 years. I had to pull my bicycle through a narrow mountain trail which leads to the cave, where one can only walk. It was so because one Sadhu told me to go that way, and he did not feel the need to tell me about another path where I could have cycled my way up. The perceptions of giving directions in different places are different. While in the big cities, we tend to be more precise and scientific. In small places, the directions are given on an emotional basis. To cut the story short, I found the cave.

Tatwale Baba's cave. In conversation with Swami Shankardas ji, disciple of Tatwale Baba ji

2.7 ENTER THE DRAGON : I entered the cave and was welcomed by Swami Shankardas ji, who is taking care of the cave of his dear Guru , Shri Tatwale Baba ji. As a normal practise or protocol, I folded my hand in Namaste and bowed to the Samadhi of Tatwale Baba ji. I stood there for a few minutes like that. I immediately went into a state of bliss. My mind got empty and the thoughts ceased to flow. I could not decipher what had happened. With great resistance, I withdrew myself from that posture and the experience, so that I could begin my conversation with Swami Shankardas ji. I sat down on the floor, Swami ji was perched on top of some kind of platform. He asked me about myself and what brings me here. In the beginning, the interaction was a bit crisp and maybe a bit blunt. Slowly, we started getting synchronized with our thought processes and understanding of humanity. The conversation turned into an amazingly deep spiritual dialogue.

From 1:00 pm it went on till 5:00 pm. It had started to turn cold and dark, and I realized that I need to retreat before it turns totally dark. I

Tatwale Baba ji : 1890 to 1974

took his permission to leave with a promise to visit the next day. I stood up and again with the folded hands bowed to the great yogi Shri Tatwale Baba ji's Samadhi. Again I went into a trance. I was a bit shocked and could not prevent myself from asking about this from Swami Shankardas ji. What he told me is something I can never forget. He said that you have no questions left and your mind has become focused. I could not really understand what exactly this meant. I hurried back, my face glowing and radiating some kind of aura. I met an American on my way back whom I had met a day before. We both were actually on bicycles and had crossed each other while I was hunting for the cave. He had actually cycled from New Delhi to Rishikesh, though his bicycle was quite an ordinary one. On seeing him I stopped and told him that I am returning after an ENCOUNTER in that cave. He told me that your face is glowing and radiating some aura. I was indeed in some exalted state and I was having this experience of eternal happiness or the eternal bliss. I happily retreated to the ashram. Next day morning I met this very young Yog teacher from the ashram on the breakfast table,

I told him about my previous day's experience. He said in a very matter of fact way, that Shiv ji, what you have attained is something the whole world wants to attain. He then disappeared into the cocoon of his daily commitments. Next few days were spent drifting along the Ganges, and walking along the stimulating streets of this Yogic land. I was simply oscillating between the Ram Jhula and the Laxman Jhula. I was getting intoxicated by the vibrancy and the spirituality of this unique place. Though I can't recall much of

A small Shiv Temple where Tatwale Baba ji used to worship and meditate.

what happened in the days that followed, and perhaps it's not worth mentioning in this book. I was thinking about this experience in the cave, and thought that this may be some temporary change in my mind, and that this might wean away with time. Actually, my mind had become almost thoughtless. A day before leaving Rishikesh, I went to a temple and did the same procedure of bowing with folded hands just to observe my mind, and I realized that there had been no change in that experience. I felt good and thought maybe this is here to stay like this. I returned to Mumbai. Back home, I started analyzing why and how did all this happen. I could distinctly feel that as soon as a thought is about to be triggered, something is chopping it off, as if cutting it with a sword. Therefore, no thoughts were entering my mind. My mind was in my control for use whenever needed. If I had some task in hand, it focused on that task, or if I had something to plan and work about, it focused only on that, and everything else was denied entry. In short all the chatter and chaos had simply vanished. I also felt, at times, a bit strange or rather frustrating. I said to myself "Oh my mind, why are you empty?" Slowly, I got used to that way. My life was getting transformed rapidly. Clarity, Brevity and Focus were what came, and my processing and analyzing ability had moved to a different level. I started analyzing this whole situation and I started to get all the answers. I understood the whole process of how I reached that state of mind.

2.8 Energized, determined, motivated, and self propelled, I bounced back to Rishikesh in February 2016. Visits to this cave were the only things happening during my stay in Rishikesh. In order to check the effect of this cave, I decided to take some of the spiritual seekers from the ashrams to this cave. I told some of them, whom I use to meet during the meals, about my experience in that cave. Some of them wanted me to take them there. I too was keen to see whether the cave would have any effect on them. I also felt that if something good has happened to me, then the same benefit can also be accrued by other spiritual seekers. That is when I became the Pied Piper taking the curious seekers to this cave. You won't believe, almost everyone had some kind of out of time and space experience. Though none had the same experience what I have had, but they all felt that there are some kind of vibrations which is creating a divine affect on them. This validated my understanding about the theory of an energy field which gets created by every human. Yogis who are established in higher consciousness and are self realized or enlightened, have an aura, a highly positive energy field not just around them but also around the place they live in.

2.9 During this visit in February 2016, I met one couple from Russia in the ashram dining hall. I was noticing that they were always sitting on a separate table. I was curious as to why are they not sitting with everyone else, where we all mingle and discuss our experiences. I could not resist, so I decided to get them into a conversation. I asked them if I could join them at the table they were having lunch. They were more than happy. They also looked like very simple and nice people to me. Irony was that they could not speak English and I could not speak Russian. So we tried to converse using Google translator on our phones. Within a few minutes the man said that I should visit them in Moscow. I was very impressed and touched by the instant connection he developed with me. I also suggested to them that they should visit this cave. Next day they were planning to visit the **Vashistha Cave** which is about 20 kms ahead of Rishikesh. They asked me if I would like to join them and share the cab. I agreed and we went together to Vashistha Cave. This cave is big, deep and dark. It is very quiet over there. The only problem I observed was that it tends to get crowded. While one is trying to meditate there, but due to the constant movement of people it is not really possible to mediate there. During my visit to Vashistha Cave in the year 2018, I had a different experience. I could get the cave exclusively for myself. This is because one of the prominent politician cum sadhvi, Uma Bharati ji was visiting the cave while returning from Badrinath. She and her staff descended on this place and everyone was asked to vacate the cave. I was walking from the Ganges towards the cave complex and she was going towards the Ganges. We crossed each other and I did Namaste to her. She acknowledged and started talking to me. She then blessed me in the traditional Indian way by encircling her hands around my head. I then proceeded to the cave. The authorities thought that I was also some big personality who knew her, so they did not stop me. I always walk confidently without any doubts or inhibitions in my mind, so generally it helps to get through places. Maybe this is because of my military background. While I was meditating there, Uma Bharti ji also came inside, and both of us meditated there for about half an hour. One can feel the pure emptiness in the cave. It helps one disconnect from the outside world. It is a good experience to have, though in normal circumstances, it is almost impossible to find the cave without any visitors.

Vashishtha Cave

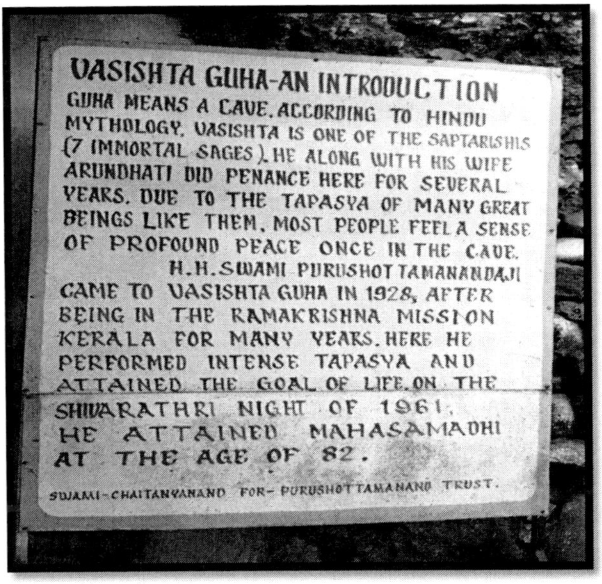
VASISHTA GUHA-AN INTRODUCTION
GUHA MEANS A CAVE. ACCORDING TO HINDU MYTHOLOGY, VASISHTA IS ONE OF THE SAPTARISHIS (7 IMMORTAL SAGES). HE ALONG WITH HIS WIFE ARUNDHATI DID PENANCE HERE FOR SEVERAL YEARS. DUE TO THE TAPASYA OF MANY GREAT BEINGS LIKE THEM, MOST PEOPLE FEEL A SENSE OF PROFOUND PEACE ONCE IN THE CAVE.
H.H. SWAMI PURUSHOTTAMANANDAJI CAME TO VASISHTA GUHA IN 1928, AFTER BEING IN THE RAMAKRISHNA MISSION KERALA FOR MANY YEARS. HERE HE PERFORMED INTENSE TAPASYA AND ATTAINED THE GOAL OF LIFE. ON THE SHIVARATHRI NIGHT OF 1961, HE ATTAINED MAHASAMADHI AT THE AGE OF 82.
SWAMI-CHAITANYANAND FOR- PURUSHOTTAMANAND TRUST.

DEVPRAYAG

2.10 After visiting the Vashistha cave, we returned to Rishikesh. We had lunch in Rishikesh and then dashed off to the Tatwale Baba's cave. Later on, we were discussing which other places nearby can be explored. By then I had heard about Devprayag, which was closest to Rishikesh, being 70 kms away. It was a two hours ride by a cab. We decided to share a cab and explore Devprayag. Devprayag is where the two rivers Bhagirathi and Alakhnanda converge, and from here the river is actually known as Ganges. It is one of the five holy prayags. Prayag means confluence. Bhagirathi is the river that comes from Gaumuh near Gangotri. Alakhnanda comes from Badrinath.

LIBRARY & MUSEUM – VEDHSHALA, DEVPRAYAG

2.11 The next day we reached Devprayag by 10:00 am. Just outside Devprayag, we stopped at a motel to freshen up ourselves. At the motel, we asked the owner if there is any real living yogis or saints in this place. He suggested that there is one place called Vedhshala (observatory), where one sadhak by the name of Acharya Bhaskar Joshi ji lives. He mentioned that Bhaskar Joshi ji meditates for 12 to 14 hours every day. This clue was enough for us. Without wasting any time, we headed in that direction. Vehicles can go up to the circuit house, from where one has to walk up a steep path. Huffing and panting, we reached his house. We were welcomed by Mr. Prabhakar Joshi ji who is the brother of Acharya Bhaskar Joshi ji. Unfortunately, Bhaskar Joshi ji was not there on that day. His brother, who is not into spirituality, mentioned that we could have spiritual discussions only with Bhaskar Joshi ji. They actually belong to the Namboodri clan of Kerala, who were moved to Badrinath to take care of the temple there. Bhaskar Joshi ji spends half the year in Badrinath temple when the temple is open. Pt. Chakradhar Joshi ji their father, was an astronomer as well as an astrologer. Traditionally, they are astrologers. Nevertheless, Prabhakar ji offered to show us around what all they have. They have a small museum or rather a personal collection of their father Pt. Chakradhar Joshi ji. He has an amazing collection over there. To mention a few things, there is this epic called Bhrigu Samihta – Collection of Leaves (Bhoj Patra). This book has a page for every human on earth, which tells us about their future and past. Then there is this entire Bhagavad Gita written on one single sheet of paper with micro or nano alphabets, which can only be read with a magnifying glass.

Acharya Bhaskar Joshi ji

Original copy of the news paper of the day when the first mission of Apollo had landed on the moon. Many obscure and precious manuscripts and books on a vast range of topics in mysticism and spirituality. A full-fledged collection of books, or rather a library. Even books in other languages like German. Last time I was there, I saw that the government had undertaken a task of digitizing those rare manuscripts. Then there are two huge German made telescopes which are not working now and need to be repaired. Sometimes I feel that there is immense precious content and knowledge available in many places in India, but now there are no takers for that. We the materialistic humans don't feel that they are of any importance to us.

2.12 After seeing the place we were offered a very delicious lunch. In fact, the food in their house is probably the most delicious food I would have ever had.

2.13 **The Out of Time & Space Spiritual Experiences in Devprayag**: After eating the food, we were relaxing independently. I was standing and gazing at a tree in the courtyard, and I got lost in that. I felt that I have lived here in my previous birth. Then I experienced something weird; that there is a pillar of fire in front of me, which is infinite in height. That fire started to get inside me and I started to feel uneasy, after a minute or so I felt more uneasy and I informed Prabhakar Joshi ji about this. He mentioned that this is some spiritual experience which only Acharya Bhaskar Joshi ji can explain. I somehow sat down on a chair and Prabhakar ji chanted some mantras, while the Russian friend Mikhail did some Reiki, which he seemed to have learned in Moscow. After a few minutes I became normal. I could not figure out what had happened and took this as a one-off incident.

2.14 In Nov 2016, during my next visit to Rishikesh, I returned to Devprayag to meet Bhaskar Joshi ji and this time there were quite a few experiences I had over there. Bhaskar Joshi ji met me and we had a conversation for around thirty minutes.

After that, he gave me a banana. I felt that an electric shock had travelled through my body. I instantly went into ecstasy. I went up to the library, where a few Europeans were also sitting. Bhaskar Joshi ji had refused to talk to them and they were looked after by Prabhakar ji. When I went there, what I saw was indescribable. They were all in some kind of bliss. After sitting in that place for some time, we all moved to the terrace, which has a wonderful view of Devprayag. Everyone got lost in their own emptiness, sitting or standing. I too was standing and gazing at the emptiness. It went on like that for an hour, and I felt that I did not have any weight. At the same time, one girl who hails from France came to me and told me that she was feeling weightless. I was shocked to hear that, and I told her that I too was feeling the same. Later, I returned to Rishikesh. I felt again, like leaving everything and moving here forever.

2.15 These incidents changed me completely. Sub-consciously, there was a rapid transformation happening constantly inside me. While there was a pull of spirituality through these experiences, at the same time there was a constant repulsion from the unreal worldly life, which had its constant challenges and struggles.

2.16 Another point to note is that every time I returned to Mumbai and joined back my office; a few of my colleagues told me, as soon as they saw me, that there is some glow around my face. Another colleague said that there not just a glow just around the face but there is a glow all around my body. This was not once but almost every time, on my return from the Himalayan sojourns, I heard this from some of them. I always ignored this, as the spiritual path is not for getting distracted with these kinds of things. In my opinion there was some energy field change which was happening as part of my spiritual evolution.

2.17 **The First Road Trip**: By 2017, I had made as many as four to five trips to Rishikesh and Devprayag. In Oct 2018, I shifted to Pune as my wife had moved to Warsaw, Poland for her new job. By then, I had decided to quit my job and pursue spirituality as a passion and profession. I too was to move to Warsaw by April 2019. In Oct 2018, I had planned a 30 days trip to explore the interiors of the Himalayas in search of real yogis. It was a project I had conceived so that I can also share the findings with the spiritual seekers. I wanted to make a proper documentary and I was hoping to tie up with the Discovery channel, but it could not materialize. I started from Pune in my car and I covered various spiritual places like Maheshwar, Rishikesh, Devprayag, Uttarkashi, Gangotri, Kedarnath, Gwaldam, Almora & Kasar Devi, then back to Rishikesh and finally to Pune. I clocked almost 6000 kms in one month. It was a very hectic and tiring trip.

2.18 **First meeting with a lady yogini in Uttarkashi**. We had the chance of meeting a yogini, Sita Devi ji who is approx 65 years old. We met her in the ashram where she had put up on her way from Gangotri to Delhi. She told us that she lived with her husband, who was an enlightened yogi. They lived in Tapovan for 20 years. Tapovan is ahead of Gaumukh and it is at a height of 4000 metres plus. It is also inaccessible most of the time of the year as it remains covered by snow almost throughout the year. Any yogi who can sustain themselves in such conditions are definitely not an ordinary yogi. We had a long chat with her and I have a video on my YouTube channel of that conversation. She discussed more about the siddhees (supernatural abilities and experiences) which get developed on the path of spiritual evolution. I don't find anything else worth mentioning about the conversation in this book. We met her at around 9 pm and she left the next day early morning for Delhi.

2.19 The next day I went to the adjacent ashram, Maa Anandmayee ashram, where I met the Swami ji in-charge of that ashram. His name is Swami

Joginder ji Maharaj. He spent his entire life with Maa Anandmayee, right from the age of 15 years. His devotion and dedication in serving the visitors was worth noticing. He himself prepared the food, tea, etc and ensured that I get everything right from morning breakfast to dinner. Actually, the ashram, Yog Niketan, where I stayed did not offer food. The conversations were long and deep, and I did not realize how the time flew for the two days I was there with him. One point I remember from his discourse which is there in the video also. He said that when we offer to God in the temple some offering, we do it out of our ego. We say that we offered this and that. God is omnipresent and is there in every particle in this cosmos. Everything already belongs to God, so how can we offer something, when in reality we don't own anything. What needs to be offered is respect and devotion. In fact we should hand over our ego to God, as otherwise we are unable to part with it. He also told me that your thoughts are beautiful and

Swami Joginder ji in the centre
Maa Anandmayee Ashram, Uttarkashi

they will spread in this world like the fragrance of flowers.

2.20 The next day after breakfast, we left for Gangotri. We reached Gangotri by evening, and it was snowing there. We quickly checked in to a motel and went sniffing around the small quaint place, which was almost empty. With the onset of severe winters with sub zero temperatures, everyone moves down and the place gets completely deserted and covered with a thick layer of snow. We took a light dinner and went to sleep early as tomorrow I had to go hunting for yogis in some caves around Gangotri. Gangotri has been a (tapasthali), a place where many yogis and saints have meditated. I was sure about finding a few. Due to the higher altitude, sometimes one can get restless in the night, and this happened to me as well. After some twists and turns, I could finally sleep. Travel fatigue and driving stress also add to the overall distress one can have at such locations. The morning was pleasant and sunny;

the light snow of the previous evening had melted. I hired a guide and started my treasure hunt. Fellow travelers who had taken lift from Uttarkashi ashram went ahead to see Gaumukh.

My spiritual horse (car) at Gangotri - in front of the hotel

Lalitha Mata ji : I walked towards Gaumukh for about 6-7 kms just to get the feel of the route and then returned to arrive at the cave of one lady yogini, Lalitha Mata ji, as suggested by my guide. She welcomed me and was kind enough to give me a hearing. We spoke about meditation, sufferings and the creation in general and our conversation lasted for an hour or more. She has been living there for the last 20 years. One can see the bliss and the grace on her face. It is not easy for women to live in such conditions. Though I have now come across many women who are doing their sadhana in the Himalayas. There are even women from countries like Germany, Russia, etc, who are yoginis living in such remote locations in the Himalayas. Lalitha Mata ji was the principal of Swami Vivekananda School in Assam. She belongs to Bangalore, Karnataka. Her earlier days were spent in America as her father worked there. The main takeaway for me from her was that whatever you do, do it selflessly. She also mentioned that one should learn only from a realized person. Only those who are self realized, are the ones, who can share with others, the true wisdom and the knowledge.

Lalitha Mata ji's cave, Gangotri (on the way to Gaumukh)

Otherwise, the knowledge is half cooked, and it is based on inexperience. Another important point to mention, that she told me was that God has created one world, but we are constantly creating our own different worlds out of our imagination and the wandering & confused mind. She visits the Gangotri temple every day around 5:30 pm, but quietly. During the winter season, she moves a little lower to the adjoining areas, which are at a little lower height. I really felt blessed after meeting her and wished that I could come again. She is a real inspiration and she has that divine peace and bliss on her face, radiating with the purity of humanity and love. In the end, she also offered me a cup of tea.

It is a fortune of a lifetime, to be able to meet such a realized soul in this world. She is a true yogi in every possible way. Living in such an austere and simple ways, totally amidst nature. This itself proves that she is a true yogi. Though the living conditions in such places are harsh, but they are overlooked by the divinity of that place. Blessings of Maa Ganga and Lord Shiva are always there to these divine souls.

2.21 **Meeting another Yogi – Shri Nargiri Padamgiri Maharaj ji – Gangotri**. As there was hardly any time left to explore more places, so we had to return to Gangotri. In the lane inside Gangotri, I saw a yogi sitting on a small kind of sit out projecting out of the lane's side wall. He had a divine bliss on his face. I stopped and bowed to him and asked him if I can have some conversation with him. He agreed to speak to me.

Yogi Shri Nargiri Padamgiri ji Maharaj

I introduced myself and told him that I am searching for yogis like you and I want to share this with other seekers, who are also searching for realized yogis, but do not know where to find them. We had a short conversation. He has been living in Gangotri in his cave for the last 20 years. He is a native of Maharashtra. He told me about his journey, how he gradually started living in Gangotri for short durations followed by a permanent stay. He meditates in the morning for 6-7 hours, and while meditating he sees the white light of a diya (wick). He said that he can continue to mediate even for longer durations, but then he prefers to walk down towards Gangotri to spend some time here. His cave is very small and only one person can live inside. I had asked him if I could visit his cave, to which he said no, as it is very small. He also mentioned that Gangotri is such a place, where one can remain immersed in eternal divine peace. The best thing is that he is one of those rare yogis who stays in Gangotri even during the harsh winters. He told me how he manages to store water, especially when the water can freeze during the extremely cold conditions. He too mentioned, which is the key take away for me that, only once you experience the truth and the real knowledge of self and this creation, then only you can share it with others. With these rendezvous with the two realized souls the day was over. The next day we had to return to Uttarkashi and then head towards Kedarnath.

2.22 **The Deadly Road to Kedarnath:** Gangotri to Kedarnath tuned out to be a nightmare for me due to the long distance and extremely bad roads. Once you join the Badrinath highway at Srinagar (Uttrakhand Srinagar and not the Kashmir Srinagar), the road after Rudraprayag was almost non existing. It was not at all possible to drive in one day to Kedarnath, so I had to halt at Rudraprayag for the night. The next day was the actual torture due to the non existing roads. Road widening work happens in the most unorganized and unsupervised way, posing so much discomfort as well as risk to the pilgrims. It was perhaps only due to the grace and blessings of Lord Shiva, I could finally arrive at the end of this road journey to Kedarnath. Sonprayag is the place from where one has to trek 19 kms to reach Kedarnath or else take a helicopter from Phata which is 50 kms from Kedarnath. I was completely fatigued and next day I realized that I am in no condition to go to Kedarnath, mentally as well as physically. Night in Sonprayag was again passed with restlessness due to the altitude issue as well as my fatigue. The next morning, I was lucky to get a booking in a helicopter. I could finally reach Kedarnath post breakfast. I have written this paragraph just to describe the ordeal I had to undergo. Once you arrive at Kedarnath, then everything changes as this place is out of the world. You can feel that you are not in any ordinary place. The view is breathtaking, and it is difficult to describe how divine this place is.

Kedarnath altitude 3300 metres approx.

2.23 **Another Realised yogi found just next to the Kedarnath temple**. After having the darshan (blessings) from Lord Shiva inside the temple, which was kind of crowded, I came outside. The helicopter ride allows only 2 hours at Kedarnath. Therefore, one has to do everything possible over there in that limited time frame. The moment I stepped out and turned right, I saw one yogi sitting down. It was an instant connection with him, and I decided to speak to him to find out more about him. Though there are many sadhus and naga sadhus around the temple, but there is a lot of difference between a yogi and a sadhu. My project and point of interest was yogis. Yogis follow the path of knowledge, meditation, and austerity. I bowed to him and started the conversation while standing there. The place was a bit crowded and it was impromptu, so I just stood and started talking. He is from Maharashtra, and has been living in Kedarnath for the last 20 years. In 2018, he was 64 years of age. The temperature there was -4 degrees.

and he was hardly covered. Whereas I was wearing multiple layers of woolens. He told me that even today in India, there are some fifteen highly realized yogis who are in the highest state of consciousness. Unfortunately, some parts of the video recording had a sound issue and that bit of the conversation is lost. He mentioned that his path is of truth and he has had a glimpse of self realization but he still hasn't got that permanent state of self realization. You can see how much glow and radiance is there on his face. The key takeaway for me was again that you do your work selflessly and there should never be I or me or fame or name in whatever you do for serving the humanity. He also told me that, no one else could ever come near him except a true seeker.

That boosted my ego, but jokes apart, it kind of validated that I was perhaps on the right path of spiritual evolution. I felt blessed to meet him, and even when I am writing about these encounters, I am getting goose pimples. So you can imagine, what aura they all have.

Surprisingly, I never heard about him again. I could neither ask his name nor about his place of dwelling. Generally many You Tubers are searching for yogis and saints and making their videos, but somehow I have not been able to find him in any of the videos on You Tube.

2.24 **The Mystery Rock – Bhim Shila**: In the year 2013, during the pilgrimage season. Kedarnath witnessed the worst natural calamity of the time. All hell broke loose and there was intense flooding. Rocks came rolling down from the mountain, going down the river Alakhnanda, razing everything adjoining the river to the ground. Everything enroute got swept away by the fury of the mountains, accompanied by the river. Long story short, entire Kedarnath was razed to the ground. One big rock, which is now named Bhim Shila, came rolling down and stopped just behind the temple.

Bhim Shila – the divine intervention

Naga Sadhus in Kedarnath

This rock prevented the onslaught the temple could have had. Nothing happened to the temple and it stood rock solid. People were washed away and few who survived the storm later died due to exhaustion and getting lost in the mountains. Divine places speak of their divinity, and it is for us to listen to the subtle voices of the divine place.

2.25 **Naga Sadhus** – Though, there were few Naga Sadhus sitting there, but in my opinion, they are highly ritualistic practitioners. As, I have been following the yogic path, therefore, there was no desire to discuss anything with them. Maybe I will try to understand their way of life, just out of curiosity, if the curiosity comes along with an opportunity. I am far from any ritualistic practices. I feel these are like cults and are followed by the masses. The Yogic approach and Jnana Marg (knowledge path) are very exclusive and different, which has actually attracted me.

2.26 By 2:00 pm I was in the helicopter on my way back to Phata, where the helipad is located. From there, we started towards Badrinath. While driving, I felt that with the kind of road conditions I will be experiencing, I will be overdoing this road trip and completely exhausting and burning out myself. Last minute decision, I reached Karnprayag, and instead of moving towards Badrinath, I drove towards Gwaldam. Thus, moving out from the Garhwal mountain ranges and heading towards the Kumaon mountain ranges. This in itself was a big circuit to be added. It was already 5:30 pm at Karanprayag, and I had thought that I would be able to reach Gwaldam by 7:00 pm. Mistaken once again, I ended up not only driving on bad roads but also driving in the pitch darkness. God only knows how I drove and reached Gwaldam safely at 9:00 pm. I am sure that God was protecting me, otherwise there was no way I could have reached there in one piece. In the night, the locals do not drive, and the whole area is enveloped in absolute darkness. There are also stories about encountering ghosts on the road in the night. One odd road side village, which we passed by, looked like a ghost village. In those three scary hours of driving from Karnprayag to Gwaldam, I crossed only two vehicles. One more thing worth mentioning was that, in this entire trip, there were no bookings made for stays, so everything was done at the last moment. In Gwaldam, I could get accommodation in a tourist guest house. There we could get the basic dinner that too was provided after taking pity on us on humanity grounds ☺. Gwaldam was just a night halt, and the next day I was to reach Almora. The view of Trishul peak is breathtaking from Gwaldam.

2.27 **Almora** I reached Almora in the evening. Enroute, there was this group of temples at Baijnath, and then Kausani was further ahead. I stopped at Baijnath. The temples were ancient and gave a very different feel. The view of the high

Baijnath

Himalayan mountain peaks from the temple complex was also breath taking.

2.28 **Almora :** Almora has many places with spiritual connections within the town as well as nearby. **Kasar Devi**, is one such place where Swami Vivekananda had meditated in a cave on top of a hill. There is a temple at Kasar Devi, inside which the deity has been placed towards the cave which forms one side of the pink coloured temple shown in the picture. Then we have the **Ashram of Maa Anandamayee**. She started her pilgrimage to Mount Kailash from here. Her husband took Samadhi here. In those days, the pilgrimage to Mount Kailash was done by foot, and the route was from Almora to Dharchula, Gunji, and Lipulekh pass, and then you entered Tibet. Nowadays, Tibet being a part of China, there is a VISA process to cross over to Tibet from India. The Indian government is finally constructing a road till the Tibet border.

कसार देवी गुफा
इस पर्वत की एक गुफा मे सितम्बर 1890 मे स्वामी विवेकानन्दजी ने कठोर
आध्यात्मिक साधनाएँ की थी। यहाँ उन्हें उच्च से उच्चतर आध्यात्मिक अनुभूतियाँ हुई थी तथा
नका मुख-मंडल दिव्य ज्योति से आलोकित हो उठा था। परन्तु जब वे आध्यात्मिक अनुभूति
शीर्ष पर पहुँचे तब उनके अंदर पीड़ित मानव-जाति की सेवा करने की एक तीव्र इच्छा
गृत हुई और वे अपने व्यक्तिगत आध्यात्मिक आनन्द को छोड़ जगतार्थ कार्य करने हेतु बाहर
कल पड़े।
KASAR DEVI CAVE
In a solitary cave on this mountain, Swami Vivekananda
erformed the most severe forms of spiritual practices in September 1890. He
ad higher and higher spiritual illuminations and his face shone with a
elestial fire. But as he reached the climax of his spiritual experiences, he
lt a tremendous urge to serve the suffering humanity and came out of his
rsonal spiritual bliss to work for the world.

I have visited Almora four to five times since 2018, and in the year 2019, I had stayed at the **Ram Krishna Mission Ashram** for a week. What I liked there, was the evening kirtans, in which the monks sing and play the harmonium and the tabla. The kirtans are quite invigorating and provide a wonderful divine stimulant to the mind. Then near Almora, there is also one of the twelve Jyotirling, **Jageshwar Dham**. It is about 40 kms from Almora. The last few kilometers of the drive is through a beautiful stretch of forest. I am planning to make my forthcoming trip to this place in July-August 2022. My plan is to live like a hermit in some remote area near Jageshwar Dham. After spending three days in Almora, and soaking in the beauty of the pine trees and the beautiful view of the high and mighty Himalayan peaks, it was time to move towards Rishikesh to end this road trip of 2018.

Maa Anandamayee Ashram, Almora

An hours' drive from Almora, there is a place called **Kainchi Dham**. Kainchi means scissor, and this place is around a bend which is like a scissor, so the locals must have named it Kainchi. Dham means abode. So the name Kainchi Dham. This place was the abode of **Neemkaroli Baba** ji. Thousands of people throng this place. During Guru Purnima, there is a massive bhandara. Bhandara is an open feast where thousands of people are served food on one particular day. Neemkaroli Baba had his followers coming from all over the world and they still visit this ashram. There are many mystical stories about Neemkaroli Baba. People like Steve Jobs and Mark Zuckerberg have also visited his ashram here. I always visited this place en route to Almora. I came across Neemkaroli Baba through one of the chanting videos of his devout follower, Krishna Das. After seeing his image, I had a strong urge to visit his ashram. This happened in February 2018. For two consecutive days I had this strong desire, and I literally had tears down my eyes. Finally I got a miraculous chance, which paved my way against some odds, and I could visit his ashram. The saints from whom I got inspired on my spiritual path had created a very strong pull whenever I came across them for the first time. None of these saints are there on this planet in their physical bodies. Almost all left couple of decades before. On seeing their images for the first time I had some undefined changes inside me.

I followed their teachings which are shared by some of the spiritual YouTube

Neemkaroli Baba's Ashram

channels. **Swami Ram's** videos on Yog Sutra were very inspiring and they guided me a lot on my path to understanding of the human life. Then it was the high level teachings of Jnani's like **Ramana Maharishi** and **Nisargdutta Guru Maharaj**, which opened up spiritual concepts in a different way. **Swami Vivekanada**, **Yogananda Paramhansa, Shri Yukteshwar Giri**, **Lahiri Mahasaya**, all have amazing teachings. They all inspired me deeply. **Maa Anandamayee**, had a different pull altogether. These super souls have inspired and transformed the humanity and are still guiding and transforming the humanity. They are like avatars and in my opinion immortals.

Maharishi Ramana Ashram,
Thirunnamalai

2.29 I have been able to travel to many other spiritual places in my quest for self realization. Thiruvannamalai which is the abode of Maharishi Ramana, house of Yogananda Paramhansa in Srirampur, near Kolkata, Shri Yukteshwar Giri ji's house which is near Yogananda's house, and then Dwarka. Recently in Mar-Apr 2022, I spent two months in the ashram of **Devraha Baba** in Vrindavan. It is said that Devraha Baba's age was 400 years or even more.

There may have been many realized yogis and saints in India a few decades ago, but now it looks difficult to find any. Though my attempt to find did take me to these places and I could find the ones I have written about in the beginning in this book. The saints of yesteryear were the ones who visibly guided the humanity. Though in my understanding there are yogis and saints whom the world is not aware of and they remain elusive to the world. Only few are fortunate to discover them.

Arunachala Hill, Thiruvannamalai

At present, the ones who are the popular God man are not really yogis or saints of that order, which were there a few decades ago. Though masses keep flocking to their spiritual kingdoms, but in my understanding, these God men of today are nowhere near the level of saints and Yogis I have mentioned in this book.

2.30 **Vrindavan**, an Experience in Itself: If I don't write about Vrindavan, then I will be unfair to myself and this book. I think it is necessary for me to give some ideas about Vrindavan, which are based on my personal experiences. India has many holy places, spiritual places, temple towns, mystical places, etc. It is a land filled with spirituality. India is unique when it comes to spirituality. It is this moral fabric of this country which keeps it going in an organized chaos way, coupled with some unique and amazing vibrations.

If I try to count or list the places, I will be doing an injustice, as I am bound to forget or be unaware of many such places. In fact, during my spiritual trips, I realized that one can actually find saints and yogis everywhere in this country, provided one has the right discriminatory abilities and one is making sincere efforts in searching for these souls.

Coming back to Vrindavan.

Vrindavan is one of the major religious places in India. Brij Bhoomi (Bhoomi means land) is what it is popularly known as. Land of Krishna (Brij Bhoomi). Vrindavan is a satellite town just 10 kms from Mathura. Mathura is where Lord

Krishna was born. Around Mathura there are many villages which are up to 40—50 kms away from Mathura. These villages are all part of Lord Krishna's life time in this area.

Barsana, is the village of Radha, Gokul is nearby and this is where Krishna grew up during his first few years of childhood. Gokul means home of cows (go means cows and kul means home). Then there is Gehar van (van means forest), Vrindavan, Nandgaon (Gaon means village), Radha Kund, Govardhan (the hill) – which was lifted by Lord Krishna on his finger. So this whole area is sacred and all has a long story connected to Krishna's Leela (Leela means play or acts).

This land is a land of devotees, to be precise Krishna and Radha devotees. This is the best place for practicing Bhakti Yog. People throng the place and you can be left spell bound at the sight of an ocean of people and their devotion towards Radha- Krishna. Here the locals while passing by always greet you saying "Radhe Radhe" or Jai Shri Radhe.

Therefore, even for a spiritual seeker on the Jnana path, it is good to observe and practice Bhakti Yog in Vrindavan. This is because the all four paths of Yog help in

Vrindavan, near Devraha Baba Ashram.
Tree under which I meditated

the spiritual elevation of a person. While how does one practice Bhakti Yog, is left to the individual and there is no compulsion to follow any pattern. The beauty of spirituality in India is that one is free to practice any form of spirituality. The spirituality is so vast, as good as infinite, and that is why there are infinite number of ways to move on them.

Therefore, there is no need to get acknowledged about how and what are you doing or to show anyone what and how are you doing. The spiritual journey is a very personal experience. Though many evolved beings, yogis, saints become an inspiration to the seekers, so as to give some direction and clues to the seekers.

This whole stuff just flows undefined and it appears like an unorganized chaos. Things keep happening and no one realizes to a large extent where are they heading to.

Vrindavan has numerous temples, the famous ones are Banke Bihari, Radha Vallabh, ISKCON (Krishna Balram Mandir), Prem Mandir, etc.

The place has its own buzz and vibes. One is best on one's feet while navigating on the road as well as the narrow ancient lanes. The city makes us realize that this really is an ancient town, possibly 5000 years old. While walking towards the Banke Bihari temple I took a lane which looked very deserted, possibly I was the only person. The lane was dotted with some real ancient structures, houses with a fort like construction, but unfortunately all in a dilapidated state. I could not understand the reason behind the sad state of these ancient structures.

The narrow crowded market lanes are such, that one has to walk zig zag in order to navigate through them. Walking towards Banke Bihari ji's temple in the evening was quite an eventful experience. The streets are dotted with numerous sweet shops selling samosas. kachori, sweets, lassi, chaat, and many other North Indian snacks. I always tried these during my ziz zag motion. I cannot forget the paan wala standing in some of the corners on the road selling delicious paan (beetle leaf), and that too just for seven rupees.

Vrindavan and Monkeys – One has to know the characteristics of the monkeys of Vrindavan. They love your mobile phones and spectacles/goggles. They are desperate to snatch them, especially the spectacles. You have to keep them inside your pockets or bags, and if you dare to wear your glasses, they are bound to be snatched away by the monkeys. They do it very stealthily. The street sides are dotted with monkeys at different elevations, altitudes, projections and protrusions in the street. They contribute immensely to your zig-zag motion. E-rickshaws are in plenty, and they zig-zag through these narrow lanes making your motion more curvilinear. The margins are extremely narrow between two objects/bodies.

My Devotional or Bhakti experience. The first temple I visited was Radha-Vallabh and I was lucky to get the front seat, and that too for two hours. I sat incessantly glued to the deities for those two hours and was mesmerized by them. I did get some divine experience of bliss. For more than a month I had not really stepped out of the ashram I was staying in. I was staying in Devraha Baba's ashram, which was on the other side of the holy river, Yamuna. A very peaceful place, completely different from the other bank of the river, where there was an infinite hustle bustle. Once I visited the temple of Radha Vallabh, my daily visits started actually to the Banke Bihari temple. Every evening for the next 10 days, I was drawn towards the Banke Bihari temple, where I spent about 10-15 minutes inside and then return to the ashram. I felt as if I was finally being called or summoned, and was given an opportunity to have the darshan (view) of the deities, Radha - Krishna.

My suggestion to the spiritual seekers for Vrindavan is that, take an apartment on rent or stay in MVT (ISKCON) guest house. Rental is a good option if you want to be there for a longer time. There is a lot to explore and experience there, whether you see from a bhakti angle, or a yogi/Jnana yog angle. One should visit all the nearby villages like Barsana, Gokul, Nandgaon, Radha-kund, Govardhan, etc.

I somehow had restricted myself to an experience of seclusion, therefore, I hardly ventured out of the ashram. I hope to cover the places I could not cover on my recent visit in the month of Mar-Apr 2022.

I will cover the ashrams in my chapter dedicated to the ashram experience. That is why I am not adding anything about the ashrams of Vrindavan. One more thing to highlight is that, the government has started to run the air-conditioned electric buses, which are neat and good. One can use these to visit the nearby villages. Like Mathura to Vrindavan, there is a bus every 10-15 minutes. One can check the time table at the Vrindavan bus stand.

I would also recommend that one should try to read about the teachings and life of Srila Prabhupada, the founder of ISKCON. What he has done to spread the teachings of Bhagavad Gita and the associated Bhakti Yog for the spiritual upliftment of the humanity world over is remarkable. While most people view ISKCON as a Bhakti movement, but the entire teaching is actually Jnana yog. Actually, the Bhagavad Gita itself is an epic about Jnana Yog. Jnana Yog is nothing but the understanding of the philosophy of Karma & Dharma.

2.31 In addition to the spiritual places I visited in the Himalayas, the other spiritual places I visited can be listed as follows, (especially since my spiritual exploration begin in 2015) :

- Thiruvannamalai – 2018
- Dwarka - 2018
- Auroville – 2018
- Srirampur near Kolkata – 2018
- Maheshwar, MP – 2018 & 2019
- Ujjain – 2016 (during Kumbh)
- Belur Math, Kolkata – 2017
- Wawel castle, Krakow – 2018

Wawel Castle, Krakow, Poland

Standing near the entrance to the Wawel Chakra stone

2.32 **Wawel Castle, Krakow, Poland :** In July 2018, during my trip to Europe on a holiday, I happened to visit Krakow for a special reason. I came to know that in Krakow there is something called the Wawel Chakra. The legend is that, Lord Shiva threw seven chakra stones on the earth; one of them fell on the Wawel castle, which is in Krakow. This was quite amusing. In fact, Europe has faced two world wars, so possibly, many ancient structures might have been razed to the ground. Warsaw the capital of Poland was 80 percent destroyed in the World War II. I feel that the traces of the Vedic civilization and Sanatan Dharma have got wiped out. However, if one does a thorough travel and search, some traces might still be available. One needs to do a deeper research to come out with some substantive findings. This is one aspect I would be keen to do, but I am not sure how can I do that in this lifetime. A thorough study can reveal a lot about the real history of the Vedic periods, before any religion was formed.

Then relating that to the modification of the cultures and the traces of the Vedic times in their present forms would definitely be an interesting study. If someone can sponsor me, then perhaps I can undertake that.

2.33 I reached Wawel castle in the morning around 11:00 am. The castle is really majestic, on top of the hill and facing the river, Wisla. The backdrop is breathtaking. It was summer time, so the weather was fantastic by European standards. I also came to know that the staff in the castle does not talk about the Wawel chakra and the legend behind it, due to obvious reasons. I went around the castle and saw it in its full glory from different angles. Later took a boat ride also to get a view of the castle from the river. I politely and through whispers enquired from one old staff member about the chakra stone, and there I was granted the clue. Reached there and saw few people just standing near the entrance to some place which has been kept locked. I spoke to two of them, and one of them told me that he comes here every week to get positively charged. I too stood near the door for about half an hour or so. I felt a strong pressure on my forehead after I moved away from the door. I could not make anything out of that, but the physical experience was too conspicuous to be ignored. The mystery only got more mysterious. That's why this science and the mysteries of spirituality are so deep, like a black hole where neither one can enter nor can one escape once entered.

Maybe one day the enlightenment will come to me and I will get the entire knowledge about this creation. Till then keep hunting, wandering, and sniffing. That is why I call it a "Treasure Hunt".

Maheshwar, on the banks of holy river Narmada, near Indore, MP

Maheshwar is a beautiful small town, that was the capital of the famous Queen of Malwa, **Rani Ahilyabai Holkar**. She was not just a queen but also a highly spiritual and religious person. She was an amazing and generous ruler too. Her contribution towards the upkeep of the various important Hindu temples in India is a chapter in itself. She also established a cottage industry by moving the skilled workers to Maheshwar, where a handloom unit was set up. Maheshwar sarees are famous in India. They also make shawls. There are three beautiful temples within the palace complex. One should read more in detail about her as she was one inspirational personality who could make a human out of you.

Maharani Ahilya Bai Holkar

CHAPTER-3

ASHRAM EXPERIENCES

3.1 I have stayed in many ashrams within India. Even outside India, in Poland, I had the experience of staying in ISKCON, Czarnow, near Wroclaw, and Haidakhan Baba's ashram, in Lancekorona, near Krakow. Both in the mountains, in the southern part of Poland. I will write a little bit about the ashrams I have stayed in, and in the end, give a summary about the whole ashram experience in a nutshell.

3.2 **Yog Niketan, Rishikesh**: My first experience was in Yog Niketan ashram, where I stayed during my first visit in the year 2015. This ashram is very well located, right next to the Ram Jhula tempo stand. A very serene and quiet ashram, an ideal place for a spiritual holiday. It thus became my choice of stay till 2017. This ashram offers, a morning

Yog Niketan Ashram, Rishikesh

meditation class and a morning yog class, and the same is repeated in the evening. There is also a library which has a good collection of books on yog.

The staff has been there through thick and thin and they are very polite. Participation in the ashram routine of meditation & yoga is not compulsory. The daily tariff is all inclusive of food and stay, as well as the regular classes. Food is alright too, though not the best. Some teachers have good experience and some are young. Overall it was a good deal. Since 2017 onwards or in 2018, I noticed changes in the ashram and it became more business oriented instead of spiritual oriented as new people in the trust descended after the passing away of the earlier senior trustee. Swami Yogeshwarananda was the founder Yogi. By now I had tested a lot in Rishikesh, and was keen to explore the offerings in the other ashrams.

Swami Ram Sadhak Gram, Rishikesh

Swami Rama

3.3 **Swami Rama Sadhak Gram, SRSG, Rishikesh** : I was an avid follower of Swami Rama's lecture series on Yog Sutras. There are around 85 short videos on Yog Sutras on YouTube. I decided to try out this ashram. This ashram is near to a smaller ashram set up by Swami Rama himself, called Sadhana Mandir. SRSG was set up by his disciple, Swami Ved Bharti. This ashram has better facilities as well as excellent food. The patrons are much more spiritually evolved. Though it is not located in the spiritual hub, but one will not feel like going out once inside this ashram. There is a book shop too. Swami Rama had written quite a few books. Living with the Himalayan Masters is very interesting and is quite like the "Autobiography of a Yogi". The ashram teachers are more experienced. They also conduct long duration courses of six months to two years long. At present, the Swami heading the ashram is designated as the Director of the ashram. I once saw him going somewhere in his Mercedes. If

Kriya Yog Ashram, Rishikesh

Meditation Hall, Kriya Yog Ashram

anyone wants to meet him then you have to meet his secretary to seek an appointment. There is a system of getting initiated by the followers. Though, I was never approached for getting initiated.

3.4 **Kriya Yog Ashram, Rishikesh** : This ashram is situated at the Tapovan tempo stand on the main Badrinath Highway. The main Kriya Yog ashram is in Orissa. Food is just alright. The rooms are decent and clean. There is a big meditation hall and the structure is dome shaped. This ashram has many rooms. The building has three floors and is in a circular pattern. Center of the building is the meditation hall. The ashram does not have much open space. It being on the main road, the outside is a bit noisy and crowded. Though inside, it is peaceful. Overall, it does not really give a feel of an ashram. The tariff is reasonable. So overall it is not a bad option. I had the opportunity to see the chief Swami of this chain of ashrams. He was having his lunch in the dining hall. He was served lunch in a silver plate with silver cutlery. He was served by one of the swamis living here in this ashram. The chief Swami lives in Orissa but comes here whenever he conducts some courses. Majority of his followers are from Europe and more so from France. His close disciples are a few women from East European countries whom I found to be very rude towards the ashram staff. Though, I observed that the ashram staff was very kind and cooperative. So there are many upsides and downsides in most of these ashrams. If anyone is visiting these ashrams for short time then it is fine, as the inside rumblings of the ashram management do not impact you in your spiritual state of bliss, which the package offers to you.

3.5 **Omkarananda Saraswati Ashram, Rishikesh** : This ashram is not open to the visitors for a stay. This is more of a private property where the three Swamis live. All three are originally from Switzerland. They moved to India almost 30-40 years ago, when their Guru, Omkarananda Saraswati, passed away. Omkarananda Saraswati left his body while he was in Switzerland. Swami Vishweshwarananda ji told me, that they were asked by their Guru to go to Rishikesh and buy as much land as can be possible in order to set up schools and colleges. This was with the view of providing quality education to the children in the hilly areas of Uttrakhand. Therefore, this ashram has many properties in Rishikesh as well as in the interiors of the Garwhal Himalayas. These are being used as schools for the local villagers, managed by the villagers only. In Rishikesh, they have a prominent school, and a college for Management & Technology called OIMT. Many of the large properties are rented as hotels. Many shops are there belonging to them in the main market area. Many apartments and villas in Rishikesh, which are also on rent. Many properties, like temple complexes, are rented out as Yog schools. Therefore, the Swamis are getting the required funds from the rented properties itself. This fund is used to run the numerous schools they had set up. Therefore, there is no need to do anything more than this.

Kamaksi Devi Temple, Omkarananda Saraswati Ashram

The ashram has a staff of ten to twelve personnel. The ashram has a beautiful temple of Kamakshi Devi. Every evening there is Aarti, and visitors are welcome too. Though not many people are aware of this ashram, it being on a road is not frequented by visitors or locals. It is on the bypass road to Badrinath. I spent three month in that ashram as I was welcomed to stay permanently and serve the ashram. My main task was to resolve their issues with different government offices in Uttrakhand. The Swamis here follow karma as their ideology.

Swami Omkarananda Saraswati was a disciple of Swami Shivananda, who was a self realized yogi. Swami Shivananda's ashram is just right ahead. Swami Shivananda had taken a Samadhi in the presence of his devotees and followers. There is a video of this available on the YouTube.

The head mahant of this ashram is Swami Vishweshwarananda, then Somshekhari ji, she is a renowned Bharatnatyam dancer. The youngest of the three is Swami Satchitananda.

Gita Bhavan Ashram, Rishikesh

3.6 **Gita Bhavan, Rishikesh** : This is another different kind of spiritual wonder on the planet RISHIKESH. This is closer to the concept of an ashram, as it is actually free for the visitors. This is entirely funded by the wealthy business class Marwari community. The Marwari community is a native of Rajasthan, but they run traditional businesses all over the country. Like most of the sweet shops, mom & pop grocery stores, etc are owned by them. They are very traditional in their way of living; they are much closed as a community. Something funny I noticed about them. They seem to be living on a very rich diet, as was evident from the dimensions of the women folk from their community. They walked, as if their bodies are moving simultaneously in all the directions, while they drift ahead. The food provided in this ashram is very pure, very simple and made in pure ghee. It is very reasonable just for fifty rupees and unlimited helpings. The ashram premises are very well kept, the ashram is right on the banks of the river Ganges. One can donate whatever one can feel one should give, or may not donate anything at all and can stay for free. It is open only for the Indians. There is no prior booking and one has just go there and try your luck. Single people are not allowed. They have seven different complexes. One of the complexes has apartment concept where you can stay in an apartment. Just a double storied system. There is no restriction in the duration of stay; you have to comply with the ashram guidelines. The rooms also have attached kitchenette and you can borrow utensils and cook your own food. The only thing which bothered me there was the high volume of the loudspeaker ranting out the discourses or Ramayan, day in and day out. This actually disturbed the peaceful ambience, which the ashram could have otherwise provided. So this makes it difficult to get a proper environment for a good spiritual experience. As the cost of food is so cheap many people not living in the ashram also come to eat and the queue becomes very long and you have to eat along with all kind of hungry people on the same table. This is where one has to see what can be acceptance in reality. It is like a test of pure form of acceptance and tolerance.

3.7 **Gayatri Parivar, Shantikunj :** This ashram is located just after you enter Haridwar coming from Rishikesh. I stayed here just for a day. This is actually not the main Gayatri Pariwar, this is the breakaway faction of the AWGP – All World Gayatri Pariwar. The Guru who had started the Gayatri pariwar, was **Pandit Sriram Sharma**. He was an amazing yogi cum saint. His teachings and discourses are so wonderful and potent. They are hard hitting, straight and to the point. He was like a strict teacher and preacher. He was a highly self realized yogi. There are many stories which can be read in his books. There is a YouTube channel also managed by the ashram.

Effective and meaningful
preaching is one that is
presented not by a speech,
but by its conduct.
—Shriram Sharma Acharya

This ashram is really good. It is there on my radar to have a longer stay. The organization does a lot of social work apart from spiritual efforts and initiatives. I would say that one should just listen to the lectures of Gurudev, Shriram Sharma. They are like pearls of wisdom.

3.8 **Ramkrishna Mission Ashram, Almora** : I stayed here in Oct 2019 for eight days. This ashram has its headquarters in Belur Math, Kolkata. I was fortunate to stay even in Belur math once during my official trip to Kolkata in the year 2018. I wanted to understand this mission and what does it offer to the followers or anyone who wants to be part of it in some way or be a part of the organization. This mission has ashrams all over the world, and it is one of the most organized and structurally well managed entities. It is also a purely pro Bengali dominated organization. Most of the monks join the organization at a young age and grow within. They get posted to different ashrams. There is a

Vedic university in Belur math. Swami Vivekananda was its founder. Swami Vivekananda was a master of Vedic knowledge and a yogi of the highest order. His teachings and his life are most inspiring and if followed sincerely can transform a person spiritually. The monks here sing beautiful bhajans in the evenings. Though they are not very forthcoming when it comes to staying in the ashram. My request had reached there through the Belur Math headquarters. I realized that this is another protocol oriented bureaucratic organization, maybe it is needed to be like that to preserve its ethos. We always view everything to suit our needs.

3.9 **Devraha Baba Ashram, Vrindavan :** This is my latest experience, where I stayed from 24th Feb 2022 to 18th Apr 2022, almost for two months. Devraha Baba was a highly respected saint who left his body in the year 1990. He is known to be 400 years old, some say 250 years and some say 900 years.

He was born out of the river Sarayu and took Samadhi in the river, Yamuna. There are many tales about his mystical ways. I do not want to list those stories here. He lived on a tree house on the banks on the river Yamuna. It is here that his Samadhi/memorial was built by his two disciples. They also started an ashram for Baba's devotees over there. At present the disciple Devdas ji also known as Bade Maharaji ji is the ashram head. The ashram has daily kirtans in the morning and in the evening. There is free food everyday for all the visitors, all the three meals. Ashram has a three storied building with approximately 60 plus rooms of different size and tariff. There is a (Gaushala) cow shelter with approximately 500 cows. Bade Maharaj ji meets visitors from 2 pm to 5 pm. This ashram is located away from the rumblings of Vrindavan, as it is on the other side of the river bank. There is absolutely no habitation around it, so the outside is very serene. Though inside the ashram there are enough hustle bustle of people and the various rituals being carried out by the ashram priests. The crowd here is raw and not really spiritual in the way you would like to see or be with, so this ashram is more so for the devotees of Devraha Baba who are more rustic and largely from the nearby villages. Then there is always an element of politics of the management trustees, which was a big turn off for me. The dining area is unhygienic. Somehow I find it difficult to define, as to what this ashram can offer.

Devraha Baba, Samadhi Sthal, Vrindavan

3.10 **Maa Anandmayee Ashram, Vrindavan** : I stayed here for 3 days from 21 Apr to 24 Apr 2022. They do not give for more days until and unless you are connected with them or if you are a Bengali. Maa Anandmayee trust just like the Ramkrishna Mission trust is also totally dominated by the Bengalis, and they are quite pro-Bengali. This is what happens to most ashrams after the saints leave their body. This trust has many ashrams all over India, but in my opinion the condition of these ashrams is declining. There is hardly any pre-defined activity and most visitors are old time followers of Maa.

Therefore, these ashrams are not really a place for the spiritual seekers. Point here is that if you are purely into Bhakti Yog, then one can choose these ashrams in Vrindavan. If you are seeking spiritually, then you will prefer a very serene set up and surroundings. Himalayas provide that serene surroundings and uplifts you spiritually.

Vrindavan has too much crowd and one has to be deeply immersed in Bhakti to navigate through that crowd and still find that solace. I hope you understand what I mean.

Ganges, Uttarkashi

3.11 **Maa Anandmayee Ashram, Uttarkashi** : I have visited this ashram twice, enroute to Gangotri in Oct 2018 and Oct 2021. Just spent a day or two. It is a small ashram with just four rooms for the visitors, and few rooms for the sadhus. The Swami Joginder ji who is approximately 68 years old, has been its caretaker. Now the trust has appointed some young monk, threatening the existence of Swami Joginder ji. He is a great person and serves the visitors with great devotion all by himself. The Ashram is right next to the river Bhagirathi (Ganga ji).

3.12 **Auroville, Pondicherry** : I guess everyone knows about this place. It is a concept where the world is borderless. People from different parts of the world have been living here. I liked the ambience and the vibes of this place. It has been kept in a very natural way, making one live closer to the nature. They also have a large meditation centre. Maa Aurobindo and her philosophy, is what is being followed over there. Ma Aurobindo was originally a French person; therefore, this place has many French origin people. Pondicherry itself was a French colony, therefore; it is natural to find French people here. I would recommend this place for pursuing

Auroville

the spiritual practices or choosing this as a place to live. They have certain policies based on which one can decide whether it fits into your needs or not. This is a good place for the spiritual beginners who do not want to go deeper into certain ways of the spiritual life. This place provides a simple and peaceful living. It also provides ways to keep you occupied in running the various areas/facilities of the ashram. One can actually be gainfully occupied in serving and managing the whole place, as done in a community. Maybe I will visit again to experience it more deeply. My earlier visit in 2018 was very short, just for two nights.

3.13 **Mirtola Ashram, Jageshwar Dham, near Almora :** I visited this ashram in Apr 2022 while I was in Almora for a week, as someone told me about this ashram. This is a beautiful ashram about 8 kms before Jageshwar Dham, near Almora. This ashram seems to be open only to the followers of the erstwhile Spirltual Gurus of this ashram. It was started by **Maa Yashoda**, who moved there with her follower called Krishna Prem. **Krishna Prem** was a UK Air Force fighter pilot who flew in the World War, post which he moved to India. Later the third person to arrive there was also from the UK Air force, an aeronautical engineer by profession. He took over the reins of the ashram after Krishna Prem passed away. Nowadays, there is just one lady by the name Chitra Iyer, living there and managing that ashram.

Krishna Prem

Ma Yashoda

The story is quite complex. I don't think that this ashram has an open door policy for the spiritual seekers. I could not understand why do they even call it an ashram. Maybe this ashram is only for the social elites who feel the call of the spirituality. Anyway, it is all up to the founders to decide what policies they make and what do they want to do over there. How are these ashrams funded or are they self funded, is quite an interesting aspect to understand. It is better to stay away from trying to understand the working of these ashrams. Nevertheless, it is one of the most beautiful ashram one can live in for their spiritual practices. They have a huge expanse of land where they grow many cereals and vegetables. The ashram has employees to look after its infrastructure. I would say that, this is kind of a private ashram, and I think that, it is fine to keep it this way. One has to first get associated with the ashrams, and then see the possibilities and opportunities.

3.14 Kabir Smarak, Village Luniya Khedi, Muxi, Ujjain

Padam Shree awardee Shri Prahlad Singh Tipaniya is a folk style singer of Kabir Bhajans. He has performed internationally and spread the teachings of **Sant Kabir** far and wide. I had the fortune of being at his place for three days in Sep 2021. He has built a Kabir memorial over there.

CHAPTER-4

TEACHING EXPERIENCE

4.1 During my stay in Yog Niketan ashram in Rishikesh, I met many seekers from different countries and made many friends. The discussions over the lunch and dinner, gave me a peek into their view points as well as an insight into their desire to visit Rishikesh to understand Yog. I was pleasantly surprised to see that the ashram was filled only with the seekers from other countries. I always found myself to be the only Indian there. Though this has changed rapidly in the last two three years, and perhaps, now the ratio has changed in favour of the Indian seekers. Corona also played a spoil sport in altering the whole scene.

What alarmed me was that though these seekers from other nations were coming to Rishikesh with some hopes and expectations of gaining some good knowledge about yog(yoga), but they were not really getting what I felt could have been provided to them by these ashrams. The reason being, that the ashrams were only offering which I would consider to be a very basic package of Yog asanas and some adhoc unknown meditation class. Though the whole life style was a good experience, but it missed what a real ashram could have offered.

21 days of meditation teaching in Costa Dorada, Spain. The students were posing for a picture and tried to show that how awestruck and confused they were with this philosophy class. The first five days were bewildering after which they realized the depth of this class and became calm.

What were lacking were the element of spirituality and the teachings of the Vedic science by an experienced Guru. There are no experienced or realized Gurus or sadhaks who could impart such knowledge. The ashrams had left the teachings of the founder Gurus limited to his books stacked up in the ashram library and one idol of the guru in the yog hall. There was no one to take the seekers into the teachings of the founding guru. Therefore, the legacy of the Guru was only there as a brand for enabling the ashram to run as a profit centre instead of a spiritual centre.

I felt sad and could empathize with these travelers coming from the far off lands, who spent a lot of money just to come all the way to India to take a dig at yog and spirituality. Ironically these travelers were also not aware of the lack of offering, and they returned in a way I would say partially satisfied. For them this experience itself was radically different from what they experience in their western homeland.

As I went through my own spiritual evolution and rapid transformation, I also felt that I can take the element of spirituality to their shores. Seeing so many westerners travelling to India, I got curious to understand how yog is being practiced in the European nations. I decided to explore this. As I was travelling to Europe almost every year, I decided to put a dip stick to check the viscosity of the Yog practice in Europe. In July 2018 I was travelling to a few countries, Hungary was one of them. This was my second trip to Europe. In my first trip in the month of Mar 2018, I had spent only three days in Budapest. I had liked Budapest so much that I decided to visit again for a longer duration. So this time I was there for 8 days. Before starting this trip, I had written to a few yog studios asking them, if they would be interested in getting a meditation workshop conducted by me in their studio. One studio agreed and I conducted two workshops. The response was very encouraging. The participants were thrilled to get to know this aspect of meditation.

This gave me headway to take this forward and I decided to organize a few more workshops. I was fortunate to be able to organize in the beginning of 2019 two full day workshops in

Geneva, Brussels, Czech Republic, Antwerp, Costa Dorada and Warsaw. In Costa Dorada it was actually a 21 day course. As I had moved to Warsaw, Poland, I continued with this in the form of regular classes in one of the big studio, as well as at my home. I also had a few individual students. The beginning was good and feedbacks were very encouraging, thereby, validating what I was sharing. I was also invited by one museum in Warsaw "Museum of Asia Pacific". They use to conduct regular events and I could give a talk on my spiritual journey. I gave a presentation cum talk, followed by many questions from the inquisitive audience. I was to give more talks there but then this covid came and everything came to a screeching halt, which I took with a pinch of salt. In this onslaught by corona most yog studio got closed for ever. I returned to India in Nov 2020, as my wife wanted me to remain employed. So I took up a job and all my spiritual life came to a grinding halt. I hope to start teaching again as I enjoyed it thoroughly and it was really a blissful experience to be teaching. Especially, when I saw the effects of

Meditation Philosophy Class in Geneva, Mar 2019

Meditation Philosophy Class in Brussels, Apr 2019

teachings, I got a further boost to continue it. I am not sure how will my life unfold but it really does not bother me. Last two years life has been on a roller-coaster. My plan was to shift from Pune to the Himalayas and set up a spiritual centre for the serious seekers. I had seen a few places where I would have liked it to be set up, but as of now it remains a dream. Though a YouTube channel happened and then book writing, so I feel that the mediums to reach out to the seekers get created and the flow does not stop. Circumstances are a constant happening in one's life and are also constantly changing, but the target should remain steady. Then there is always a possibility of our intentions (not expectations) getting fulfilled.

Links to the You Tube Channels

1. The first channel link :

https://youtube.com/c/ShivMathur

2. Second channel link :

https://www.youtube.com/channel/UCaQUcMJtPtYabcNyeUfbcgA/featured

3. Third channel link :

https://www.youtube.com/channel/UCkMnv-jf00M400FuICB-TUQ

CHAPTER - 5

YOU TUBE CHANNEL

5.1 In March 2020, in Warsaw, during the lockdown I had all the time in my life. The Himalayan road trip of 2018 in which I had met and recoded my conversations with some Himalayan Yogis, were yet to be converted into a documentary. My project partner was just not getting time and always had some reason for not being able to do it. I neither had the plan to do all this video editing myself nor did I know how to do it. My wife suggested and then insisted that why don't I do it myself. Under duress and with all the time to myself, I attempted to edit, but I could not really edit and then without much of editing I just uploaded two three videos on the YouTube. One fine day, sometime in May 2020, one of the video, of Lalitha Devi ji got recommended by YouTube and it took off. That's when I realized that this is actually the beginning of a channel. So from no plan to have a YouTube channel, Thereafter, I uploaded more videos. Tatwale Baba's video was made in August 2020. It needed a lot of translation work and therefore, hours went in to creating it. Moment it was uploaded it took off as well.

5.2 Then I started to upload my own videos on meditation and spirituality. It was also a request from some of my acquaintances in Warsaw, that I should upload videos of my meditation classes. As it is not possible for many to be able to come and attend my classes.

5.3 As on June 2022, I have a total of 72 videos on my channel with almost 24K subscribers and 4.2 million views.

5.4 Way ahead – Since April 2022, the channel started to take a beating and I felt that I need to do something to keep it going. As such, I was always analyzing the data points from the YouTube analytics. I found that, most of my subscribers came from watching the videos of Himalayan yogis and also that YouTube does not recommend all the videos on the channel. It is advisable to focus on a particular niche. I had uploaded videos in five different categories. Here what I got was followers of Himalayan yogis videos and not the followers of meditation or spirituality videos. Therefore, I am now doing a restructuring of the channel. I am creating separate channels for Meditation, Spirituality, Devotional music (chanting/kirtans/bhajans), Spiritual travels, and the Himalayan yogis. I am also working on different formats of the video making and editing.

5.5 The idea is that I should build up a base of content for the seekers of this knowledge and experience. It is very important to give back to the society. When you look back in life, you will have no regrets of not giving back to the society any skill you possessed and which is of benefit for the masses. I only wish that I can make good content which can give some direction to the spiritual seekers in the times to come. It is like being on a mission.

"**Not a Mission Impossible**"

Maybe Tom Cruise will come and help me here in this Endeavour.

CHAPTER - 6

SITUATIONS IN LIFE

6.1 This is the most sensitive chapter of this book. I was not sure whether to have it or not. So I am writing itas of now, and will decide later whether to keep it or remove it. It will depend on what gets written here, based on that, I will take a decision.

6.2 The most challenging situations of my life were the ones which made me start searching for the realities of life. These situations made me pause and look back and look around. They triggered my questioning process so as to slowly awaken me from the deep slumber I was in. I was living in the darkness covered by the veil of ignorance, under the influence of materialism, consumerism and hypocrisy of the modern society. Attachments galore, social targets all over the mind and the body, I was running without a pause. I finally stumbled and then I got up, dusted myself, and then started to remove the dirt of ignorance and the dirt of modern day upbringing accumulated over my mind.

6.3 When someone close to you turns around and leaves you in the middle of your worldly chase, you are totally taken aback by the turn of such events. You wonder that, while you take all the troubles for the people around you, but one day the same people can no more be there for whatever reasons. That is when, you question, that for whom and for what, are we always into a wild Goose chase.

What is needed in life? Who belongs to us? How do other people survive and manage their life?

6.4 Many situations of betrayal come into one's life. These make you withdraw away from all the close ones. Inadvertently, It leads you to a door of solitude and detachment, and if you do not enter this cave of detachment and solitude, you will inevitably suffer from the attachments and the expectations of the materialistic society. I also realized that, all the relationships are purely transactional and opportunistic in this era of kaliyug. Lust for materialistic needs and desires, is the only overriding factor. That is when you decide to tread on the spiritual path with more clarity.

6.5 There is no point in being very explicit explaining my personal situations here. I am only trying to bring out the fact that one can go through unimaginable challenges in life, and instead of seeing them as a suffering, view them as a lesson and move in the direction they are supposed to take you. Resistance to happenings is the biggest cause of miseries in the worldly world. Acceptance is the need.

6.6 The important thing to note is that, due to my experiences in the spiritual world and my attaining of certain state of mental awareness; I am able to go through everything without any fuss and sufferings. To me there is nothing like sufferings. To me the only thing which matters is Karma and Dharma.

6.7 Tough situations and challenges in life are nothing but another kind of experience. They make you an all rounder. Life is supposed to teach you constantly and it makes you grow, otherwise you will go away like a half baked dish.

CHAPTER – 7

THE AUTHOR JOURNEY

7.1 I was not very inclined to write a book, but writing a book was suggested to me by a few of my acquaintances. I did understand at one point that, it would be a good idea to write a book so as to document my teachings and experiences. This is good not just for posterity, but it also puts all the scattered knowledge in an organized way and in one place. Print medium or the book as a medium is still a big medium to expand the reach of my experience sharing. I was alone in Pune from May 2022 onwards as my wife had again joined a school in Mumbai. I realized that I have all the time, tranquility and uninterrupted space available to make this book writing happen. I was never a reader of books, so writing was never in my dream, as far as two months back. Though the idea of writing did pass through my mind once in a while, but it always got sidelined, due to my lack of inclination or love for the books.

7.2 Around 10th of May 2020, I got down to writing the first book, whose cover image is there above. First three days I could write 3 to 4 pages, and I was told that, it was fine at that speed. Not interested in the norms of book writing, I decided to pick up pace, as I wanted to finish this and then start my travel. I could write 30 pages every day, and by 20th May 2022, I had finished the book. It was self published on 25th of May 2022 by a publisher called Notion Press. Then I went on to publish again through self publishing mode with (KDP) Kindle Direct Publishing in USA, Draft2Digital in USA and Lulu in USA. This way the book's e-book and paperback version both could be made available globally. I am now scouting to get it published through some big time publisher in India who also has a global reach. I am more concerned about the print quality of the books sold in India, and its distribution in India. Notion Press is unable to provide a good print quality, and distribution is non-existent in their dictionary.

Through “Findaway Voices”, a publisher who has a tie up with the publisher Draft2Digital, I am able to publish my audio book version also.

I am also looking at the video format. In fact I have made a video of chapter-1 and uploaded that video on my YouTube channel. Here is the link to that :

https://www.youtube.com/watch?v=D3dhNrl9gIM&t=6s

After publishing the first book, I felt that I should also document my spiritual travel experiences. This was also suggested by a few of my acquaintances. The writing seem to have become an addictive habit and unstoppable too, therefore, the second book also took birth. As this book got published on 13 July 2022, the concept and desire to pen down the third book had already taken birth (actually typing on the computer though I would love to write my script with an ink pen). Second book was completed in one weeks time. This time I spent more time in editing the script. I have done three rounds of editing. Apart from editing which is a very tiring exercise for the brain, the formatting which becomes a parallel and a continuous need, further adds to the woes.

Cover designing is another tricky game, especially when it comes to uploading the right format as per the specifications of the publisher's portal. Therefore, when you are trying to write a book, then what follows is few rounds of editing, proof reading, parallel formatting, cover designing and then uploading and publishing on the portals.

How my last three months flew by, I have no idea. Time became irrelevant. Only thing I feel sometimes that if I can put myself on a medical drip, then I can perform the act of book writing without a break. Food breaks and other daily chores do cause a break in this act of book writing which is nothing less than a flooding river, where the flow does not seem to stop and is willing to inundate everything enroute. I hope my books inundate the readers and the masses, while it peeps out of the windows on the bookshelf of the quaint book shops in the streets of every town.

CHAPTER - 8

LIVING WITH THE HIMALAYAN YOGIS

8.1 I have added this chapter intentionally in this book, but the content is not yet ready. As part of my spiritual journey this aspect is waiting to happen and my mind is all geared up to experience this aspect of the spiritual life. I have been practicing and working on solitude, detachment and renunciation since quite some time. Situations in life are also acting as an enabler.

8.2 Travel is on the cards, but somehow getting delayed as I decided to finish with some of the unfinished tasks like writing and publishing the two books, restructuring the YouTube channels and get them rolling with enough content for the hungry seekers. I am hoping to get these behind me by the end of August

2022. Once all is in place, I should make this move of going to some remote place in the Himalayas and live like a yogi and do my sadhana. In the beginning I want to live with a yogi which can be helpful for me to settle down with whatever support one may require there.

8.3 **Therefore, I am showing this chapter which is likely to be a chapter in my life, but at present it is blank**. I hope you will all forgive me for including a blank chapter in this book. I think, I must be the only person to have a chapter in the book but without the required content. It is like a silent movie. So bear with me, if everything goes well, then the content for this chapter will appear and reach the readers. For the time being, let it be a mystery. It is like, who killed Katappa in the movie Bahubali

8.4 After all the ashram experiences, it is time to go beyond these ashrams, which are a different kind of worldly place, and cannot take you beyond a certain limit, in your spiritual journey. Many people comment like a wise person, that one need not go anywhere and can get self realized anywhere. To such advisors I have this answer, ask all the yogis who went to the Himalayas that, why did they go there. Second answer is, that, while you are giving this advice, have you got yourself self realized or even wiser to some extent.

Samadhi

The Final Objective

CHAPTER - 9

THE FINAL OBJECTIVE

8.1 The final objective is to attain complete detachment – Vairagya. Getting into the state of Samadhi. Samadhi is a state of constant Bliss. It will come naturally after attaining complete detachment. Along with the complete detachment, the ego also has to wean away completely. Total surrender, perform the karmas, serve the echo system within your capacity and potential.

8.2 It is a long journey and there is no known time frame to reach this goal. Whether this goal will be achieved or not in the present birth, is also not known. It is important to have a target in this journey, and make constant and gradual efforts towards that goal. There is no hurry to reach there. One should move with the right balance of everything in life. There is a time for everything. When the intentions are right and there is sincerity in the efforts, then it is likely to happen. Patience is needed. There should not be any burden in the mind about achieving this.

8.3 All the situations in our life teach us. Life is like a book, with many chapters full of everything. Be it romance, be it a thriller, be it a mystery, or drama, or sadness, or the traumas, etc. The list is endless. We do not study well and we keep failing in the spiritual exams, thereby, getting stuck in junior classes. Though the time flies and the age catches up, but many are unknowingly stuck in the primary class. Time does not stop, and this journey of being in a book called life comes to an end. One opportunity lost, the soul continues its journey in different forms, and sometimes back in the human form where it gets another opportunity to get liberated. This is the science of creation, created by the Universal supreme power, which we call God. God is formless, and when you get into a Samadhi state, then only you realize the presence of that Supreme. Has anyone really tried to understand, what is this creation. It is nothing but the science of existence and transformation of the energy with consciousness as the basis. Consciousness is nothing, but the omnipresent connected energy. It moves in between different kind of physical forms and invisible mediums, connecting everything. Once this can be experienced, then only one can experience oneness with everything.

There is energy in everything and energy gives life. What is tangible to the humans, as a living being, is not just the life form, but one has to see the life form in every particle of this creation, including the ether.

Swami Vivekananda

Maa Anandmayee

INSPIRATIONS

Saints and Yogis who inspired me with their life, their teachings and their experiences:-

Guru Nanak

If you can read and understand Guru Granth Sahib, then you don't need any other literature in your spiritual path. If you want to see spirituality, then visit the Gurudwaras.

Sant Kabir

If you listen to his poems, which are sung by many folk singes like Prahlad Tipaniya or Prakash Gandhi. They will also be enough to move you on your spiritual path. I am a regular listener of Kabir bhajans. His words are lethal.

Acharaya Shriram Sharma ji

I have watched his speeches which are very potent and straight. I love his hard hitting and meaningful talks. They will open up your closed mind.

Tatwale Baba ji

Neemkaroli Baba

Nisargdutta Guru Maharaj

Swami Rama

Shri Yukteshwar Giri

Parmahansa Yogananda

Ramana Maharishi

Acharya Bhaskar Joshi ji

TRIBUTE TO TEACHERS AS GURUS

Prof PG Sastry, 10 Jul 2022
Hyderabad.
I was fortunate to meet him at his residence.

I am also having a photograph of one of the most eminent professor my college had. Teachers are no less than a Guru. Some of them are so distinguished in their field that they are a big inspiration as well. The way they have devoted their life to their field or subject with dedication is beyond comparison. They have set benchmarks with their knowledge, dedication, humility and simplicity. One should seek guidance in all walks of life from them. They can be an epitome of inspiration in a very holistic way. Though I was a student of Electrical Engineering, but I am paying respects to Dr PG Sastry being a flag bearer of our college, due to his immense contribution to this field of Engineering in numerous ways.

Prof. Dr. PG Sastry. He was the most eminent professor in the department of civil engineering in the National Institute of Technology, Warangal, India. He also became the principal of the college from 1990 to 1992. He has many designations which I cannot even remember or list down here. No irrigation project gets implemented in the country without his approval and his designs. He did his research work in Fluid Mechanics, in the Gothenburg University Laboratory in Germany.

My likely Next book

Title : Social Pandemic

Sub-title : A Terminally ill Modern Society

Printed at Repro India Ltd.